Face to Face

DRAGONS

Dougal Dixon

tangerine press

an imprint of

SCHOLASTIC

www.scholastic.com

Contents

A gargoyle keeps watch

Q2AMedia

Created by Q2AMedia
www.q2amedia.com
Text, design & illustrations copyright © 2009 Q2AMedia

Editor Katie Dicker
Publishing Director Chester Fisher
Art Director Sumit Charles
Senior Designer Joita Das

Client Service Manager Santosh Vasudevan
Project Manager Shekhar Kapur
Illustrators Subhash Vohra and Aadil A. Siddiqui
Art Consultant Jonathan Downes
Picture Researcher Shreya Sharma

Tangerine Press edition copyright © 2009 Scholastic Inc.

an imprint of
SCHOLASTIC
www.scholastic.com

Scholastic and Tangerine Press and associated logos are trademarks of Scholastic Inc.

Published by Tangerine Press, an imprint of Scholastic Inc., 557 Broadway, New York, NY 10012

Scholastic New Zealand Ltd.
Greenmount, Auckland

Scholastic Canada Ltd.
Markham, Ontario

Scholastic Australia Pty. Ltd.
Gosford NSW

Scholastic UK
Coventry, Warwickshire

Grolier International, Inc.
Makati City, Philippines

10 9 8 7 6 5 4 3 2 1

ISBN-10: 0-545-13010-7
ISBN-13: 978-0-545-13010-3

Printed in China

Beowulf, the greatest monster killer of all

What are Dragons?

What if all the stories about dragons were true? Let's look at some of the ancient stories and legends, and you can decide for yourself.

Long ago, huge, magical animals were said to roam the world. According to different cultural myths, some of these creatures caused untold damage, yet others protected people and helped control the weather. Every ancient civilization had its dragon stories.

Dragon types

There are a lot of dragons in films, comic books, and TV. Although they differ from one another, most have a body like a giant snake, lizard, or other animal; many fly with powerful wings. Ancient stories and legends describe different types of dragons. There were dragons that destroyed villages, while others guarded great treasures of gold, silver, and gemstones. Most dragons had awesome magical powers. Some even brought luck and prosperity to the people who found them.

⏶ The Eastern dragon is the exact opposite of its Western counterpart. It is the keeper of wisdom and has a gentle nature.

▶| *The Western dragon has teeth, claws, wings, and a scaly body. It is known for its evil disposition.*

The teeth and claws of Western dragons are like those of fierce animals, such as lions or crocodiles.

An Eastern dragon is often shown with the antlers of a deer and the scales of a fish—both creatures that we think of as being gentle.

Strength and power

Dragons were often used as a badge or a symbol of strength and power. A knight with a dragon on his shield, or a pirate with a dragon figure on his ship, was showing the world how big and brave he was.

Evil Dragons

The Western dragon was one of the most dangerous animals that ever existed. Its aggression toward people and civilization is legendary. These dragons could be found all over Europe.

St. George, the patron saint of England, is one of the most famous dragon slayers.

Essence of evil

Dragons may have looked different from each other. The number of legs, number or type of wings, skin color, even the number of heads varied, but the feeling of evil that came from these creatures was overwhelming. The wrath of an evil dragon could destroy whole villages and leave the people in fear. A rumor of a dragon in the area would quickly spread as people did all they could to defend themselves.

Fights with knights

Evil dragons were powerful and almost indestructible. They could only be defeated by the bravest of heroes. Many people rose to the challenge to test their strength against these dangerous creatures. Most perished, but some triumphed and passed into history. Old paintings show these epic battles.

▼ *The Western dragon streaks through the sky with batlike wings, raining fire and destruction down on helpless villagers. It is a terrifying sight and strikes fear into those who see it.*

Heroes and Dragon Slayers

Some people don't believe that Western dragons ever existed, but because they symbolize all the evil in the world, it is widely thought that only a person who is pure of heart can destroy a dragon.

St. George was not the only dragon slayer. In the 6th century, St. Samson fought one dragon in Wales, another in Cornwall, England, and two in Brittany, France. He holds the record for defeating the most dragons in a lifetime!

St. Serf, traveling across Europe from Rome, met a dragon in central Scotland. He defeated it and then settled in Scotland, setting up communities in Fife.

▶| *Throughout history, revered men such as St. Serf were said to be so pure of heart that they had the power to defeat dragons.*

St. Petroc defeated the last dragon of Cornwall in the 6th century. He threw his cloak around its neck and whispered a prayer in its ear. The dragon swam out to sea and was never heard from again.

In the south of France, a group of townspeople killed the Tarasque, a local dragon, after St. Martha had tamed it. Afterward, the people were sorry for what they had done. They renamed their town Tarascon in memory of the dragon. Today, an annual parade is held in its honor.

◀| *On the last Sunday of June each year, the people of Tarascon, France, parade through the streets with a full-sized model of the Tarasque.*

11

The **Lambton Worm**

Some stories tell of a dragon's revenge on the people who tried to slay them. Lord Lambton was one of these victims.

Hundreds of years ago in Durham County, England, young Lord Lambton went fishing instead of attending church on a Sunday. One day, instead of a fish, he caught a very ugly worm with nine holes on each side of its head. It was so ugly Lord Lambton threw it down a well.

Many years passed and Lambton, having forgotten all about the ugly worm, grew up and went to fight in the Crusades. But the worm grew, too! It escaped from the well and began to terrorize the area by eating all the animals that crossed its path. After it had eaten every creature in sight, it wrapped itself around Penshaw Hill (or some stories say Worm Hill).

Descriptions of the time say that the Lambton worm crawled around at night looking for prey.

▶| *The Lambton worm grew from a little worm to a monster that could wind itself several times around a hill.*

A lasting curse

When Lord Lambton returned, he saw the damage the worm had caused. A wise woman in the village told Lambton to cover his armor in spikes to defeat the dragon. Then, she instructed, he was to kill the first living thing he came across after the dragon was dead. When the worm tried to wrap itself around Lambton to crush him, it was impaled on the spikes and died. Unfortunately, the first living thing Lambton came across was his father. He just couldn't kill him, so the family was cursed for nine generations.

▲ *The dragon was so big it could wind itself seven times around Penshaw Hill in County Durham.*

They say the worm had big teeth, a big mouth, and big eyes.

The worm would feed on calves and lambs, and would swallow children alive.

Its terror was so great that news of it reached all the way to the Middle East where Lord Lambton was fighting in a war.

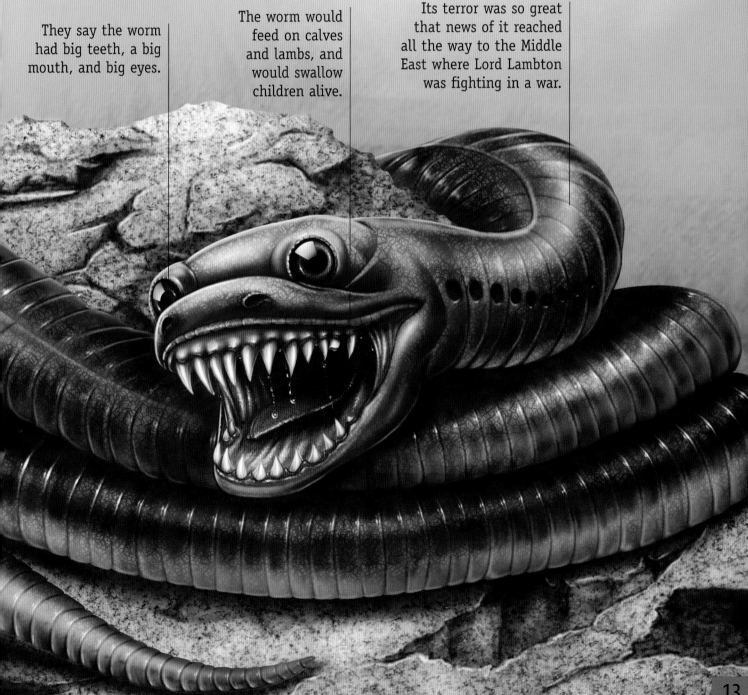

13

More Dragons' Revenge

The Knucker

A dragon called the Knucker lived in the Knucker Hole, a pool near Lyminster, in Sussex, England. It was causing so much trouble that the local authorities offered a reward to anyone who killed it. A local man, Jim Pulk (or Puttock) managed to poison the beast. But he, in turn, was killed by contact with the dragon's poisonous blood or from the poison that was used to kill it. His death remains a mystery.

The dragon and the dog

Sir Peter Loschy was a knight who fought with a dragon near Loschy Hill in Yorkshire, England. His faithful dog came to help him, but the dog became contaminated with the monster's blood during the battle. Sir Peter died after the dog licked his face in celebration of the victory.

Another story tells of a dragon terrorizing Kellington in Yorkshire. Ormroyd the shepherd killed the dragon, but Ormroyd died after being licked by his dog, too. Could these two stories be the same event?

The teeth were long and sharp, like those of a meat-eating reptile, such as a crocodile.

Dragons' wings were like bats' wings rather than birds' wings—flaps of skin supported by long fingers.

Many dragons had an arrowhead-shaped point at the end of the tail—possibly some kind of stinger like a scorpion's.

◀ *The name Knucker comes from the old Anglo-Saxon word nicor, which means a "water monster".*

Beowulf

In the 5th century, the greatest monster killer of all was Beowulf of Scandinavia. After killing two monsters (Grendel and Grendel's mother), Beowulf became king. In his later years, Beowulf had to do battle with a fierce dragon that appeared in his kingdom. Beowulf managed to defeat it, but was so badly wounded in the fight that he died soon afterward.

▶| *The dragon became enraged when part of its treasure was stolen. Beowulf had to kill it before it destroyed his whole kingdom.*

Dragon **Power**

Sometimes, people were more impressed than terrified by the power of a dragon. Many ancient people used the symbol of the dragon to show their own strength.

A powerful image

The wyvern was a dragon with a pair of wings and only two legs. It often held its head high. The Romans used the wyvern as a symbol of power, and around A.D. 43, the symbol was introduced to Britain. Toward the end of the first millennium A.D., Viking raiders mounted carvings of dragons on the bows of their ships to give themselves courage and terrify their enemies. During the Middle Ages, the symbol represented nobility.

When the sign of the wyvern reached Wales, the image was changed into a four-legged dragon. The Welsh dragon is a powerful symbol of nationalism in Wales to this day.

◄ *A wyvern's claws were like those of the fiercest bird of prey—the eagle.*

|◀ The majestic red dragon of Wales is a form of wyvern, but it has an extra pair of legs.

Guarding the Treasure

Dragons were known to be greedy. If they happened upon a treasure, they guarded it with all their might. It was very difficult to separate a dragon from these riches.

Today, when ancient hero stories are acted out (as in this production of Richard Wagner's Ring Cycle opera) stage effects are used to show what the dragon Fafnir looked like.

Cursed treasure

In the early days of what is now Germany, a king of vast wealth owned the Treasure of Andvari. His riches included lots of gold and a very special red gold ring. The king's greedy son, Fafnir, wanted the treasure for himself. So, he stole it all and then hid away in the caves of Gnitahead to guard it. Fafnir's greed eventually transformed him into a beastly dragon.

The death of Fafnir

The great hero Siegfried found the dragon's cave. When Fafnir the dragon left his hoard unguarded, Siegfried hid in a hole in the cave floor. As the dragon walked over the hole, Siegfried thrust his sword into the soft underbelly of Fafnir.

The legends of dragons guarding treasure may have been created by people who wanted to keep their valuables hidden. The idea that their treasure was guarded by a dragon or a curse would deter treasure hunters from trying to find and steal it.

FACT

▶ *Killing a dragon would not only give a warrior great prestige, but could also make him very rich.*

Hercules and Ladon

The Garden of the Hesperides was a lush orchard in the far western corner of the world. In the orchard was a golden apple tree that gave the gift of immortality. These were the goddess Hera's apples, so the tree was guarded by a dragon named Ladon. According to a legend, Ladon had many heads. Hercules was given the task of getting one of the golden apples. In one story, Hercules got the apple, but had to slay Ladon in the process.

Smaug's treasure

In J.R.R. Tolkien's story *The Hobbit*, Smaug the dragon guards a treasure in Lonely Mountain (Erebor). Bilbo Baggins, the hobbit, steals a cup from Smaug's treasure, and Smaug gets very angry. No one can see a way to kill the dragon because Smaug's soft underbelly is crusted with gems and gold. But Bard the Bowman of Esgaroth finds the dragon's weak spot and kills it. Smaug was one of the last dragons of Middle Earth.

Smaug, the keeper of the treasure in The Hobbit, *is one of the most famous of storybook treasure guardians.*

Jason and the Golden Fleece

One of the most famous Greek stories in history is that of Jason and the Argonauts. In this story, the people of Colchis hung a sheep's fleece of pure gold in a tree, which was guarded by a dragon. Jason and his crew killed the dragon to retrieve the Golden Fleece.

▶ *The people of Colchis, on the southeastern corner of the Black Sea, treasured a golden fleece that was hung in a tree. They set a fierce dragon to guard it.*

River Dragons

Some dragons liked to live in damp, dark places. Some lived in water, which is why they were rarely seen. This added to their mystery and put people in fear of lakes and rivers.

Long ago, in the deep waters of the River Seine, in France, lived a huge snakelike dragon called the Gargouille that regularly sank riverboats. Sometimes, the dragon would come up so quickly and with such force that the waves would flood villages and surrounding farmland.

The Gargouille had a long neck, a narrow snout, and eyes that glowed like jewels.

▶| *When St. Romain defeated the Gargouille, he had its head mounted as a trophy on the tower of the cathedral of Rouen in France.*

In architecture, a gargoyle is a water spout, usually carved in the shape of an ugly animal. It gets its name from the water dragon Gargouille.

Although the Gargouille was tamed by St. Romain, the local townspeople killed it. This event was similar to the story of the Tarasque, also in France (see P. 10–11). Events like these led to the decline and the ultimate extinction of dragons.

As a water animal, the Gargouille had limbs that were quite small and only used for steering. It was the writhing motions of its great body that caused the waters of the river to surge and flood the land.

The **Hydra**

Dragons were always difficult to kill. They were not immortal, but some had magical powers and properties that made them almost invincible.

⌃ *The labors of Hercules were so famous that the ancient Greeks illustrated them on temple walls and vases.*

In ancient Greece, there lived a multi-headed dragon called a *hydra*. It lived in the swamp that surrounded Lake Lerna. Some stories say the creature had nine heads, one of which was immortal. Other stories insist that the hydra had hundreds of heads. Every time a head was cut off in battle, two more grew back in its place.

Hercules fought the hydra with his nephew Iolaus. Every time Hercules cut off a head, Iolaus burned the stump of the neck with fire to prevent another head from growing. Hercules buried the immortal head under a rock. Like many dragons, the hydra's blood was poisonous. After the dragon was dead, Hercules dipped his arrows in the blood to make them lethal.

Whether it had nine heads or several hundred, the hydra would have been a difficult monster to subdue.

Some people think the hydra was actually an octopus. An octopus' eight tentacles were thought to be heads on necks, and the octopus' true head was the immortal one.

FACT

◀ Hercules was cursed by the gods, and had to carry out 12 labors to make up for the bad things he did as a young man. Some of these labors involved killing monsters, such as the hydra.

Dragon's Teeth

One day, Cadmus sent a man to a nearby spring to get water. When the man didn't return, he sent two more men. They didn't return either, so he sent the rest of his men. No one returned, so he went to see for himself what had happened. When he got to the spring, Cadmus saw a dragon guarding it. At first, Cadmus was afraid of being eaten, but the dragon was slow and lazy because he had eaten all of the other men.

Cadmus easily slew the dragon. Now, with no men to help, the goddess Athena came to Cadmus' aid. She told him to plow a field and sow the dragon's teeth. As soon as the teeth were in the ground, full-grown warriors popped up. The men turned first on Cadmus and then on each other. They were badly wounded, but after Cadmus nursed them back to health, they helped him establish the city of Thebes.

▼ *In World War II, stone pyramids called "Dragon's teeth" were built to defend areas of land from approaching tanks.*

▼ *The dragon that was slain by Cadmus was the guardian of a spring. In many stories, we find that dragons were associated with running water.*

Dragon **Parts**

Many dragons are made up of the parts of other animals. Sometimes they have the properties and abilities of those animals, too.

Griffon (or Gryphon)

One of the best-known dragons is the griffon. This powerful creature has the body of a lion, and the head and wings of an eagle. As a mixture between the king of the beasts and the king of the birds, the griffon is a magnificent creature.

It originally comes from the East, possibly India. Legends tell of how the griffons found gold in the mountains, built their nests out of it, and terrorized anyone who came near.

FACT

In central Asia, the dinosaur fossil of a *Protoceratops* is often found. This was a lion-sized animal with four legs and a beaked skull, like that of an eagle. People who don't believe in griffons think that the story of the griffon came from discoveries of these fossils.

The head of the majestic griffon was the head of an eagle but usually with feathery ears.

The front feet had eagle's talons.

The back legs and tail were the hindquarters of a lion—king of the beasts.

▶| The griffon had magical powers. Its claws could heal the sick, and its feathers could restore sight to the blind.

The opinicus was related to the griffon, but you could always tell them apart because the front legs were more like the legs of a lion than the legs of an eagle.

Opinicus

An opinicus has the legs of a lion and the tail of a camel. This is the beast that is frequently seen in heraldry, or coat of arms. Sometimes it is shown without the wings, and sometimes its name is spelt Epimacus.

Hippogriff

The hippogriff was like a griffon, but it had the forequarters of an eagle and the hindquarters of a horse. Unlike the griffon, this was a very gentle animal and often used as a symbol of love. It appears in children's novels, such as the Harry Potter series and *The Book of Dragons*.

Shirrush

The shirrush featured a lion's forequarters and an eagle's hindquarters, in addition to its snakelike neck and tail. Tales of the creature came from the area of modern-day Iraq. Pictures of the shirrush made from colored tiles, decorate the walls of the ancient city of Babylon, along with bulls and lions and other animals.

Chimera

The chimera came from the eastern Mediterranean. It had a lion's body, a snake's tail and two heads—one of a lion and another of a goat. It was said to be a fierce, fire-breathing creature. Modern zoologists use the term chimera to mean an animal made up of parts of other animals, such as a dinosaur skeleton that is put together with the bones of different types of dinosaurs.

The famous chimera terrorized the area of Lycia in the Middle East and was defeated by the Greek hero Bellerophon.

If Looks Could Kill

Dragons were very powerful. Some were able to kill or stun their victims just by looking at them. Others simply used their deadly breath.

The basilisk

The basilisk was one of the most famous dragons known for its deadly stare. Basilisk lore described the creature, which was hatched by a rooster from a snake's egg, as part snake and part rooster with a crownlike plume of scales. However, an exact description is not known, because no one who ever laid eyes on it lived to tell the tale! Because it was so deadly—just a touch was enough to kill—the basilisk symbol was used in heraldry, decorating flags, and shields. This identified the knight as someone who was brave and dangerous.

◄ *This stained glass window from Basel, Switzerland, has a coat of arms featuring two basilisks—symbols of strength and power. A basilisk with wings is usually called a* cockatrice.

▼ *The basilisk was extremely dangerous—its deadly stare and highly toxic breath caused almost instant death to those who fell in its path.*

The head had a plume of scales, like a rooster's comb or crown. *Basilisk* means "little king".

Its powerful eyes could cause death by a single glance.

Its pungent breath would leave you gasping.

The basilisk did not even have to touch its victim to kill him.

The Guivre

The Guivre from France was a water monster built like an enormous snake, with the horned head of a dragon. Its toxic breath was deadly and shrivelled any vegetation that it passed. What's more, the effect was long-lasting, leaving deadly plagues in an area whenever the Guivre emerged from the water.

The Guivre was finally defeated when it accidentally caught sight of a man without his clothes. The Guivre was so shocked that it could not attack, and was soon expelled from France. Some say that the monster went to the north, where people wear a lot of clothes!

Poisonous breath is common among dragons. But it was the Guivre that had the deadliest influence of all, spreading diseases throughout medieval France.

Some people think a dragon's killer breath is a story based on the venomous bite of some snakes.

FACT

The cockatrice was able to fly with its wings.

Its body had scales like a reptile.

Its birdlike feet had sharp, dangerous claws.

The cockatrice

The cockatrice resembled a basilisk with wings: It was hatched by a toad or a snake from an egg laid by a rooster. The cockatrice first appeared in the 12th century, but was extinct by the 17th century. This creature was a particularly dangerous type of dragon. Some could kill people or turn them to stone just by looking at them. Others killed prey with their poisonous breath.

In Wherwell, Hampshire, England, a cockatrice was trapped in a monastery. The local people offered a reward to whoever could kill it. A man called Green came up with the idea of presenting the cockatrice with a mirror. Its deadly look reflected back at itself and Green was able to kill it.

The cockatrice was like a large rooster with a lizardlike tail. It could kill by looking, touching, or breathing on others.

Sea Dragons

Even today we do not know much about the animals that live in the depths of the oceans. According to ancient legends, these areas are home to some fearsome creatures.

The Kraken

The most famous sea dragon was the Kraken of the North Atlantic Ocean. This creature was so big that it would seize ships and drag them to the bottom of the ocean. As the Kraken surfaced, it would strand ships on its islandlike back. As it submerged, it created whirlpools that sucked the ships down. Even though fishermen knew of and feared the Kraken, the shoals of fish that accompanied the great beast kept them coming back to sea.

Those who claim to have seen the Kraken told of an animal that was part octopus and part crab. It first appeared about A.D. 1250, but by the 18th century, the description became more and more like a squid. It may be that those who first saw the Kraken actually saw a giant squid. Seafaring was hazardous at the best of times, and it may be that many ships that disappeared mysteriously were victims of the Kraken.

Modern squid can reach great sizes, but none has been seen that was as big as the Kraken.

Lurking at the bottom of the sea, the Kraken waits to pull a ship to its doom.

Dead whales that wash up on beaches are often unrecognizable. The rotting blubber falls away from the carcass, and the waves roll it up into strange monsterlike shapes. Also, when an enormous basking shark dies, its huge jaws drop off leaving a tiny skull. This makes the corpse look like a small-headed, long-necked sea beast, such as the extinct plesiosaur.

FACT

⬓ *Ancient mariners knew so little about the life of the sea that they were willing to believe in sea serpents.*

FACT

Sea monster sightings could be based on glimpses of real sea animals such as whales or giant squids.

Cetus

Ancient Greek legends tell of Andromeda, a princess who was chained to a rock as punishment for her mother's vanity. Andromeda was sacrificed to the sea monster, Cetus, who terrorized the coastal regions of the eastern Mediterranean Sea. The Greek hero Perseus rescued Andromeda and then turned the monster into a rocky island by exposing it to the sight of Medusa's severed head (a woman who could turn people to stone by her look).

The sea monsters of Troy

In the same region, toward the end of the Trojan wars, two sea serpents emerged from the ocean and carried away Laocoon, the Trojan priest of the sea god Poseidon, and his two sons. There is some confusion about the reason for this. Some say it was because Laocoon warned the Trojans of the Greeks' plan to sneak into the city walls inside a wooden horse to capture the city of Troy. Others say that it was a punishment for destroying a sacred shrine.

▲ *In old maps, the seas abound with many monsters.*

Eastern Dragons

The Eastern dragons of China, Japan, and Southeast Asia were majestic creatures with sharp claws and dangerous horns, but they have always been known as symbols of money and good luck.

A good luck symbol

Eastern dragons were very special. These wise and powerful creatures were known for bringing good luck and the rains for a plentiful harvest. These water-dwellers called lakes, rivers, and seas their home. Many temples were built to love, worship, and honor Eastern dragons.

Japanese dragons

In Japan, it was believed that many rulers descended from dragons and could change themselves into dragons. The Japanese emperors decorated their palaces and clothes with dragon symbols, including their robes, thrones, and boats. If an emperor was called "dragon face," it was a big compliment.

Statues of dragons are often found outside temples, shops, and restaurants to bring good luck.

Row of sharp spikes.

Thick, hard scales.

Sharp, curved
horns like
a deer.

Slithery,
snakelike
body with
no wings.

Razor-sharp
talons like
an eagle's.

Soft belly not
protected
by scales.

Chinese dragons

There are nine types of Chinese dragon. Each has different powers and appears on different paintings and carvings. They are:

A noisy dragon, carved on bells and gongs.

A musical dragon, carved on musical instruments.

A book-loving dragon with its image found in libraries.

A very strong dragon, carved at the bases of columns.

An alert dragon, carved on the eaves of temples to warn of danger.

A water-loving dragon, carved on bridges.

A restful dragon, carved on thrones.

A fierce dragon, found on the hilts of swords.

A quarrelsome dragon, carved on prison gates.

These dragons first appeared in China, and the symbol quickly spread to other parts of the Far East. The dragons make an appearance at every Chinese New Year Festival as a symbol of good luck and prosperity for the coming year.

The first Chinese dragons had four toes, except for the imperial dragon of the emperor, which had five. As the Eastern dragon moved to other countries, it lost some toes. The Japanese and Korean dragons have just three toes on each foot.

◀ *This dragon will be part of a Chinese New Year celebration to bring good luck for the year ahead.*

42

Other Eastern dragons

In India, the dragon is called Naga. It, too, is regarded as a spirit of nature. At times, it appears as a giant snake with many heads. Sometimes it grows legs, and is very similar in appearance to the Chinese dragon.

In Thailand and Java, the Naga lives underground. In Laos, it is a water animal, looking after the spirits of the rivers. In Cambodia, it is a water creature with many heads. Along the Mekong River, people still appeal to the Naga for a safe trip before setting foot in their boats.

In India, the Naga is a serpent that lives under the sea. It is said to be full of wisdom.

Dragon Facts

What did dragons eat?

Dragons tended to be omnivorous—they ate anything. Any community that had been ravaged by a dragon in the past will tell you that it ate all their cattle and sheep, and also their crops. Dragons took great joy in eating a young woman as a meal. History is full of stories of maidens put out as a sacrifice to a dragon.

The dragon Ouroboros also had an unusual diet. It ate itself, tail first! The dragon devouring itself was known to the ancient Greeks, to the Chinese of 5,000 years ago, to ancient Egyptians, and, much later, to the Norsemen. It was often used as a symbol of things that have no end. If this self-eating habit was widespread amongst dragons, it is no wonder that they became extinct!

The Ouroboros ate itself tail first!

It makes a circle that has no beginning and no end.

◁ *The Ouroboros symbolizes life as a cycle of birth and death.*

Wearing spikes or blades on your armor is an extra defense against the wrath of a dragon.

How do you kill a dragon?

If you were a dragon slayer, how would you go about killing it? Here are a few tips:

- Show the dragon its own reflection in a mirror. This would reflect its killer stare straight back to it. This is what Green did when he defeated the cockatrice (see P. 34–35).

- Fix sharp spikes all over your armor. If the dragon tries to wrap itself around you, it will cut itself to pieces. Classic dragon slayers, such as Lord Lambton (see P. 12–13) and Peter Loschy (P. 14–15) found this effective.

- Use some poison. Skuba Dratewky, a cobbler's apprentice from Poland, fed a dragon a sheepskin filled with tar and sulphur, or quicklime. This did not kill it, but made the dragon so thirsty that it drank too much water from the Vistula River and burst.

- Sometimes it is enough just to subdue the dragon by the strength of your goodness (see P. 10–11). To do this, you have to be a very noble person.

Famous Dragons

Stories of famous dragons have been told throughout the ages. You can find more information about them in books or on the Internet.

Medieval Western dragons subdued or slain by saints

St. George's dragon
St. Samson's dragon
St. Serf's dragon
St. Petroc's dragon
St. Carantoc's dragon
St. Martha's dragon (the Tarasque)
St. Murrough's dragon
St. Romain's dragon (the Gargouille)

Later British dragons

The Lambton worm (Durham)—
    killed by Lord Lambton

Dragon of Loschy Hill (Yorkshire)—
    killed by Sir Peter Loschy

Kellington dragon (Yorkshire)—
    killed by Ormroyd, a shepherd

Knucker of Lyminster (Sussex)—
    killed by Jim Pulk (or Puttock)

The cockatrice of Wherwell (Hampshire)—
    killed by Mr. Green

The wyvern at Mordiford (Herefordshire)—
    killed by Mr. Garston

Dragons slain by northern heroes

Grendel, Grendel's mother and an unnamed dragon—killed by Beowulf in Scandinavia

Fafnir—killed by Siegfried in Germany

Smaug of Middle Earth—killed by Bard the Bowman of Esgaroth

Smok Wawelski of Poland—killed by cobbler's apprentice Skuba Dratewky

Zmay Gorynych of Macedonia—killed by Debrynya Nikitich

Tugarin Zmeyevich of Russia—killed by Alyosha Popovich

Dragons slain by the ancient Greek heroes

Ladon of the Garden of the Hesperides—killed by Hercules

Guardian of the Golden Fleece—killed by Jason

The hydra of Lake Lerna—killed by Hercules

Dragon of Thebes—killed by Cadmus

The chimera—killed by Bellerophon

Cetus—killed by Perseus

The Minotaur—killed by Theseus

Eastern dragons

Naga—the Indian dragon

Nogo—the Malayan dragon

Ryu—the Japanese dragon

Neak—the Khmer dragon

Yong, Imoogi, and Gyo—the Korean dragons

Bakunawa—the Filipino dragon

Rong—the Vietnamese dragon

Long—the Chinese dragon

Index